Up, Up, Up

by Cecilia Winters
illustrated by Amanda Harvey

Practice Decodable 3

Mc Graw Hill Education

Bothell, WA • Chicago, IL • Columbus, OH • New York, NY

MHEonline.com

Mc Graw Hill Education

Send all inquiries to:
McGraw-Hill Education
8787 Orion Place
Columbus, OH 43240

ISBN: 978-0-02-145882-0
MHID: 0-02-145882-0

Printed in China

8 9 10 11 12 DSS 27 26 25 24 23

I have the  .

kite

I have the 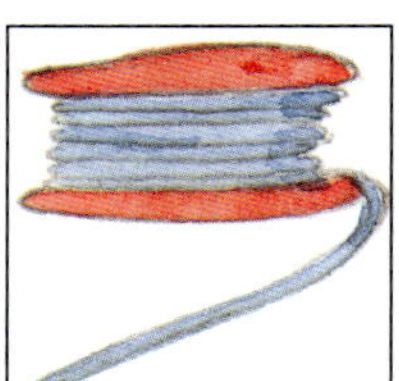 string.

The 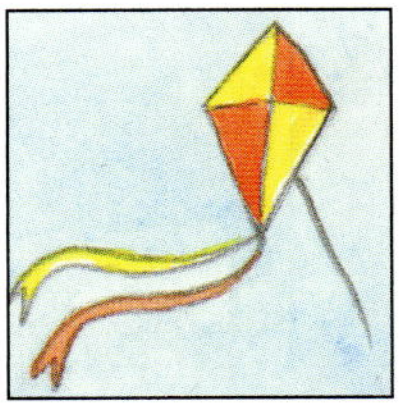 is up!

kite

The  have 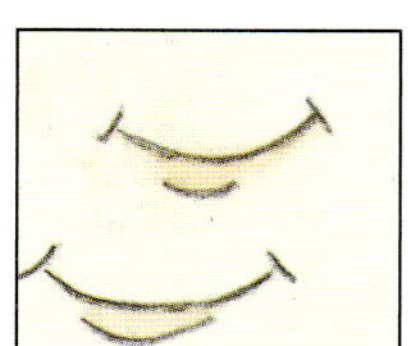.

children smiles

See the  ? I see the  !

trees trees

The  have the  !

trees kite